God's Miracle Healing
A Mother's Journey of Loss, Grief, and Healing

A True Story by Angela Frazier

"Yea, though I walk through the valley of the shadow of death,

I will fear no evil;

For You are with me;

Your rod and Your staff, they comfort me."

— Psalm 23:4

I0531269

Cover design by Forever 32 Publishing

Interior design and formatting by Forever 32 Publishing

First Edition: 2025

ISBN:

979-8-9999636-0-4 (Paperback)

979-8-9999636-1-1 (Hardcover)

979-8-9999636-2-8 (Ebook)

Published by
Forever 32 Publishing
Pineland, TX USA
For permissions or inquiries, contact:
Email: forever32publishing@gmail.com
Printed in the United States of America

Dedication

This book is dedicated to my beloved son,

Logan.

From the moment I first held you in my arms, I knew God had given me a special gift. Your light, your laughter, and your love changed my world forever.

I was blessed to be your mama for 32 beautiful years. Though your time on earth was shorter than I ever imagined, your impact will last for generations.

Thank you for showing me the meaning of unconditional love— for leaving your mark on this world, and for continuing to touch lives from Heaven.

Until we meet again, I will carry your light and your legacy with every breath I take.

Love
Mama

ACKNOWLEDGMENTS

First and foremost, I want to thank my Heavenly Father. God, you have carried me every step of the way through the darkest valley of my life. Without Your presence, your peace, and Your miracles, I would not have had the strength to share this story.

To my sweet Logan — my son, my heart, everything. Thank you for choosing me as your mama. Your love, laughter, and light continue to live on in Bryden and in every person who hears your story. I love you more than words could ever express.

To my husband, John — thank you for being my rock, for holding me when I collapsed, and for loving me through the hardest chapter of my life. Your strength carried me when I had none left of my own.

To Bryden — your daddy's legacy lives on through you. You are a daily reminder of God's goodness and the hope we hold onto. You are my precious gift from God, and I will treasure you forever.

To Amber — thank you for giving birth to Bryden, my precious gift from God. He is a beautiful reflection of both you and Logan, and my greatest blessing. Thank you for loving Logan with all of your heart.

To Lisa — thank you for being by my side through it all. Your love for Logan was deep and true, and your strength in the face of heartbreak has helped me stand when I didn't think I could.

To Cliff — thank you for being Logan's daddy and for walking this unimaginable journey with me. We have shared the deepest sorrow a parent can face, and I'm grateful we could face it together.

To Becky — thank you for being Cliff's rock through all of this. Your strength and support have meant more than words can say. For being Logan' stepmom and keeping him in line when he was with y'all.

To Debra, my prayer warrior and sister in Christ — thank you for holding me up in prayer when I didn't have the words. Your faith and friendship mean the world to me.

To Susanna, my dear friend — thank you for showing up every day to support Logan's legacy by leaving a comment on every Facebook post I've made and will make for the first 365 days. You are the one who told me to start this, and I'm so grateful you did.

To Pastor Gary Marshall, Pastor Karen Doyle Marshall, and the Harvest Church family — thank you for creating a sacred space for Logan's homegoing celebration and for walking beside me on this journey of faith and healing.

To every mama who has lost a child — this book is for you. I pray you see God's hand in your sorrow and find comfort in knowing you are not alone.

And finally, to every person who has supported, prayed for, and encouraged me along the way — I thank you from the bottom of my heart.

TABLE OF CONTENTS

AUTHOR BIO

Angela Frazier is a devoted mother to Logan, Naw Naw to Bryden, and a woman of unwavering faith. Born and raised in Redding, California, and moved to Texas in 1984, she spent her life building a home and a family, pouring love into every corner of her world. When tragedy struck and she lost her only son, Logan, Angela found herself walking through the deepest valley of grief. Yet even in that valley, she discovered the power of God's presence, peace, and promises.

Through dreams, signs, and divine whispers, Angela experienced firsthand the miracles of Heaven touching Earth. Her story is not one of despair, but of redemption, healing, and hope. Angela believes that God has given her a calling: to share Logan's legacy and help others navigate grief with grace, courage, and faith.

Angela now dedicates her life to ministering to other bereaved mothers, sharing her journey through writing, speaking, and her growing online community. She is the founder of *Logan's Beautiful Journey Home*, a movement to keep her son's spirit alive by shining hope into the lives of others.

She resides in Texas with her loving husband, John, and treasures every moment with her grandson, Bryden—Logan's beautiful gift to the world.

PART I: The Final Seven – Where Heaven Touched Earth

Chapter 1: Come See Me, Mama

It was still dark outside when my phone lit up that Saturday morning.

September 21, 2024.

A date now carved into the walls of my heart.

The message on my screen was from Logan. Just four words:

"Come see me mama."

No punctuation. No explanation. But it shook me to my core.

I sat up instantly. My heart began to race. Something wasn't right, I could feel it in my spirit. A mother knows. And in that moment, I knew—this wasn't just a casual "stop by if you're free" message. This was a cry. A calling. A spiritual alarm bell.

I stared at the message, reading it again, trying to understand what he meant. Minutes later, a second message came through:

"I had a religious experience. I talked to both sides. Scary."

What was he saying?

Both sides?

I didn't try to call. I didn't have time to process it. I just ran out the back door—Logan lived in the house behind mine—and every step towards him felt like it carried eternal weight.

When I reached his door and opened it, I found Logan lying in his bed. Pale. Disoriented. Shaken. His eyes were wide, almost distant. He wasn't himself, but he wasn't gone either. There was a flicker of something behind his gaze, like he had seen too much too soon.

He tried to explain, but the words came out fragmented and raw. He told me he had taken Tylenol PM for his back pain—that he thought he may have accidentally overdosed.

And then he began to speak of things not seen.

He whispered that the devil and his demons surrounded him. **"they told me I wasn't worthy, Mama. They said I didn't belong to God."**

But then—his voice cracked—he said God's angels came.

"And they fought for me. Can you believe they fought for me, Mama?"

And I said, **"Yes, sweetie. I can."**

His whole body trembled when he spoke. And mine did too. The room around us felt thin, like Heaven and Earth were brushing up against each other, and I was standing in between.

He kept saying,

"It was real. I saw them. I heard them."

I believed him.

There wasn't a doubt in my mind. Logan had encountered something otherworldly. Something divine. Something terrifying, yes— but also something holy. He had come face-to-face with the war for his soul, and he survived it.

But I knew we weren't out of the woods.

He told me his side hurt. That he was in pain and having trouble breathing. I begged him to let me take him to the emergency room.

He shook his head.

"No, Mama. I need to wait for Lisa—my girlfriend. She's working but will be home around five or six p.m."

I didn't understand it at the time. But something in him knew, Lisa was meant to take him.

It was part of the divine choreography already unfolding.

I placed anointing oil on his forehead and said a prayer over him. Then I held his face in my hands. I kissed his forehead. I told him I loved him.

If I had known, it would be the last time I'd ever speak to him outside a hospital room...

I would have held him longer.

But that's the thing about life-changing moments—they never feel that way when they're happening.

You don't know it's the last time until it's too late.

You just wake up one day, and the world shifts under your feet. And nothing is ever the same again.

Chapter 2: The Battle Begins

The rest of that Saturday moved slowly—like time itself had surrendered to sorrow.

Logan lay in his bed, pale and groggy, holding his side in pain. I stayed close, checking on him every hour, trying not to hover, but unable to stay away. Every time I walked back into the house, something inside me pulled me right back toward him.

There was an invisible war in the air. I could feel it in my spirit.

He wasn't just fighting physical pain. He was caught in a spiritual battle I couldn't see—but one I *knew* was real.

He told me again about the night before—how he couldn't sleep, how the darkness in the room wasn't just shadows. He said the devil had come for him, surrounding him with demons that whispered lies and accusations.

"They said I wasn't worthy," he told me, eyes wide, voice low. **"they said I had nothing left. That I didn't matter. That God didn't want me."**

And then he said again:

"But Mama... the angels came. And they fought for me."

He said it like a child remembering something too big to fully grasp, like he was trying to wrap language around the unexplainable.

He didn't know how long the battle lasted.

But he knew who won.

The pain in his side worsened as the day went on, and I begged him again, "Logan, let me take you to the ER."

But he was firm.

"No, Mama. I need Lisa to take me."

There was something in his voice knowing. Not stubbornness. Not fear. Just a quiet certainty.

She was meant to be the one.

Lisa got off work late that afternoon and headed straight home. By the time she arrived, Logan was already in his car. But something was off.

He wasn't driving. He was sitting there, confused—trying to start the ignition with his barbershop keys.

Lisa ran up to the car door and asked, "Baby, what are you doing?"

Logan didn't answer her directly. He turned his head and looked toward the passenger seat, as if someone else was sitting there.

And then he said it.

"He said we must go now. We must hurry."

Lisa was startled but stayed calm. She told Logan she needed to run to the house to get the car keys. She gently leaned him up against the car so he could steady himself while she went.

As she ran back out through the gate, something caught her eye on the ground: a large, white feather, about 12" long.

She paused for a moment and thought, *what kind of crazy bird has a feather like that?*

She didn't know about angel feathers back then. But we would talk about it later—while Logan lay in ICU.

When she returned, Logan slumped over the hood of the car. She helped him into the car and they began the drive to the ER in Jasper which was 20 minutes away.

Logan held Lisa's hand and whispered, **"I love you. Please don't leave me"**

And then he looked in the back seat and told her

"He said you need to hurry. We must get there now."

Lisa looked in the back seat, there was no one there—but she didn't question him.

She looked in the back seat as if talking to someone and said, "I'm going as fast as I can."

When they pulled up to the entrance of the ER, Lisa turned off the engine and was ready to help Logan inside.

But Logan stopped her.

"No... go to park the car. He's got me."

Lisa hesitated; Logan could barely stand on his own. But he stepped out of the car slowly. And what she saw next stopped her in her tracks.

He was leaning—on *someone*—but no one was there.

It was as if he was being supported… carried… walked into the hospital by an invisible presence.

His guardian angel.

There was urgency in the air as he stepped through those doors. His skin was yellow. His lips were blue. He was struggling to breathe.

The nurse took one look and rushed him to the back. Minutes later, Logan coded.

But the story didn't end there.

I knew deep in my soul—that Logan's guardian angel knew human intervention was required for the miracle that was about to unfold. For Logan to walk the seven-day journey God had ordained for him, he had to be stabilized. There had to be help.

And there was.

Before I even arrived, Logan coded again. The doctors shocked his heart—but they didn't have time to sedate him.

He felt it all.

And he let out a scream that rang through the ER like a siren from the depths of his soul.

God knew I couldn't have handled that sound.

So, he made sure I wasn't there for it.

While Lisa waited for me to arrive at the hospital, a kind-hearted nurse gently approached her, sensing the weight of sorrow already beginning to settle in the room. With compassion in her eyes, she placed a tiny Jesus figurine in Lisa's hand and softly whispered, "You're going to need Jesus tonight."

That small gift, so simple, yet sacred, became a powerful symbol of hope and presence during Logan's time in the ICU. That little

Jesus stayed with us through the darkest hours, and I'll share more about His significance in a later chapter.

By the time I got to the hospital, they were preparing to life flight Logan to Memorial Hermann Hospital in Houston. They knew they couldn't care for him properly where we were.

As they wheeled him out, his body barely stabilized, they loaded him onto the helicopter.

And during that fragile, in-between moment—in the air, on the way to Houston—**Logan coded again.**

Chapter 2: The Battle Begins (Continued)

When Lisa and I left the ER in Jasper and began the drive to Houston to be with Logan at Memorial Hermann, we were completely undone. Our hearts were heavy with fear and grief, and all we could say to each other was, *how could this be happening? This isn't real.*

Lisa was behind the wheel of my truck for the very first time, and even though the road ahead stretched over two and a half hours, the entire ride felt like it passed in the blink of an eye. It was as if God Himself had lifted us up and carried us to the edge of Houston—time folded in on itself, and suddenly, we were there.

It was close to 11 p.m. when we reached Houston. The traffic was backed up for miles—four lanes thick, unmoving, overwhelming. We prayed aloud that God would move the traffic so we could get to Logan. And then, just as we approached chaos, something miraculous happened. One lane suddenly opened—just for us.

It was like the parting of the Red Sea. Not a single car blocked our path as we glided straight through that sea of headlights. From the very edge of Houston all the way to the hospital, about a 30-minute stretch was nothing but a clear, open road. It felt like God was saying,

I'm making a way for you. Keep going.

When we finally reached the hospital, we had no idea where to go. We drove in circles for nearly 45 minutes, stressed and desperate to get to Logan—around the massive buildings—with not a single person in sight to ask for help. My truck is a big four-wheel drive, so we needed valet service to park, but we couldn't find one. We didn't even know which entrance would take us to Logan.

Then, out of nowhere, a police car appeared in front of us. It was as if he dropped straight from the sky. There was no side road, no parking lot, no visible way he could've gotten in front of us. He was just… there.

We sat stunned in the truck. Lisa said, "I'm going to flash the lights—maybe he'll see us." I told her, "I'll get out and ask him where we're supposed to go. Maybe he can help." But before I could even open the door, the officer quickly turned in and went back into a little space, never once noticing we were there. He didn't acknowledge us at all.

And yet, as I turned my eyes from him back to the road in front of us—just beyond where he had parked, there it was.

The valet station.

The exact entrance we needed to reach Logan.

It was like God used that moment—used that police car—to gently draw our eyes exactly where they needed to be. We weren't alone. Even in our desperation, even in our confusion—He was guiding every step. Every mile. Every moment.

We had no idea the miracles were just starting.

Chapter 3: The ICU – A Thin Place

The doors of Memorial Hermann Hospital felt cold and heavy the moment we walked through them.

But the air?

The air was different.

It was thick with sorrow… but also something holy. As if Heaven had brushed up against the walls and refused to leave. We were entering sacred ground.

Logan had arrived before us, barely clinging to life after coding mid-flight.

We rushed through check-ins and were escorted to the ICU floor. Every step down those long, sterile hallways felt like walking through a spiritual threshold. My chest tightened with every breath. My feet felt like they were moving through mud. But my heart was already in that room—with Logan.

And when I entered…

I knew.

This wasn't just a hospital room.

This was holy ground.

There was a stillness. A Hush. Like Heaven had drawn a curtain around this one place in the building and said, *"Watch. Listen. I'm here."*

When Lisa and I stepped into Logan's ICU room, the weight of reality hit us like a wave. A technician was gently placing electrodes on Logan's scalp to monitor his brain activity. He was still awake then—aware, alert, and understandably frustrated. The technician had to shave small patches of his hair so the electrodes would stick, and Logan was visibly upset because he was so particular about his hair. He was mouthing cuss words—something only Lisa and I could see—and while part of us couldn't help but smile at that familiar fire in him, it also broke our hearts.

He was trying to fight, trying to resist the loss of control, trying to hold on.

But the more he fought, the harder it became to watch. Eventually, the doctors made the decision to sedate him—for his safety, and so his body could rest.

That moment—when they administered the medication—was the last time I would ever see my baby's eyes open.

Shortly after, Logan was placed in a medically induced coma.

As the room grew quieter, Lisa remembered something—the tiny Jesus figurine that the sweet nurse in Jasper had given her. She reached into her pocket, pulled Him out, and gently tucked Jesus into the chest pocket of Logan's hospital gown. It felt right, like He belonged there close to Logan's heart, where comfort was needed most.

Later that evening, when the nurses came into clean Logan and changed his gown, Lisa walked over after they finished—and suddenly, her eyes widened.

"Where's Jesus?" she cried out, panic rising in her voice.

The nurses looked at her, confused. They didn't know what she meant.

"Jesus was in his pocket!" she said urgently.

One of the nurses suddenly gasped and said, "Oh my gosh, He must still be in the gown we threw in the dirty laundry."

Without hesitation, Lisa rushed to the bathroom where the dirty cloths hamper was. And sure enough, she found the little Jesus buried inside the soiled gown. She cradled Him in her hands like treasure, walked straight back into Logan's room, and said, "He needs to stay here… in Logan's pocket."

The next day, one of the kindest nurses we ever met came in, saw the tiny figurine, and gently lifted Him from Logan's pocket. With so much care, she took a beautiful blue cross that Cliff, Logan's daddy had brought the day before and rubber-banded tiny Jesus to it—so He'd be easier to find. Then she went a step further. She clipped the cross and Jesus to the outside of Logan's gown pocket with a large paper clip, right where everyone could see Him.

And that's where Jesus stayed.

Every time Logan's gown was changed, the nurses knew—Jesus goes with him. He never left Logan's side.

Logan and his tiny Jesus became a sacred sight in the ICU. Nurses, staff, and even people who weren't part of his care would stop by just to see Him there clipped to Logan's chest like a symbol of unwavering faith, of protection, of presence. Jesus wasn't just a figurine in Logan's pocket.

He was a reminder to everyone who walked into that room: *God is here. Still. Always.*

As I sat down in the recliner next to Logan's bed, I looked up—and there it was.

A painting hung on the wall directly across from me, just above eye level. And in the left corner of that painting… was an angel.

I can't explain it. But I knew instantly: that angel was his. Logan's guardian. The same one who walked him into the ER. The same one who carried him when he couldn't stand. The same one who had been whispering, *"We must go now. We must hurry."*

I stared at that angel for a long time. I didn't cry. I didn't speak. I just watched.

It felt like the angel was watching me too.

Like he was standing guard—assigned by Heaven, present in flesh or spirit—and I knew we were not alone.

In the days that followed, that room became more than just a place of medicine and monitors.

It became a sanctuary.

Doctors came and went, running tests, adjusting machines, speaking in hushed tones. Nurses checked vitals and IVs, updated charts, and dimmed the lights. But no matter what changed on the outside, the presence in that room stayed the same.

It was peaceful. A peace that didn't make sense.

The kind only God can give.

Sometimes I would sit silently beside Logan, just holding his hand. Other times, I would play worship music softly on my phone, letting lyrics of hope wash over him. I read Scripture aloud. I whispered prayers. I asked God for miracles. Then me and Lisa would change places, and she would do the same.

Lisa and I weren't the only ones who felt something divine happening.

The doctors and nurses began to say it too.

They'd walk into the room and pause—almost like they were stepping into a sanctuary.

Some would say quietly, "God is in this room."

Others would simply whisper, "This place feels different... holy."

It wasn't just the machines keeping Logan here.

It was something greater.

God had filled that room.

His presence was thick, tender, unshakable.

And I knew it was God's way of reminding me: *"He's still here. I've got him."*

One night, Lisa and I talked about the drive to the ER again. We were both still trying to make sense of it all.

That's when she brought up the feather.

She told me how, as she ran out of the gate to get Logan's keys, she saw this massive white feather on the ground.

She didn't think much of it at the time—just wondered, *"What kind of crazy bird leaves a feather like that?"*

She didn't know what I knew then.

She didn't know what angel feathers meant.

But then she shared something that left me completely stunned... in the most miraculous way.

She told me that two weeks before Logan went to the ER, she had a dream.

In it, the two of them were sitting side by side in rocking chairs on a porch, holding hands, watching the sun set over a beautiful lake.

She turned to look at him... and he was gone.

She woke up crying.

Logan, concerned, asked, "What's wrong, baby?"

She told him about the dream, and he looked at her with tears in his eyes and said,

"You know I'm going to die before you, right?"

She shook her head, "No, you're not."

But he simply replied,

"It's for certain… I am."

We cried together that night. Not just because Logan was in that hospital bed. But because we realized: God had been sending signs from the very beginning.

He was never out of reach.

Day by day, the ICU became a place of spiritual warfare and sacred worship.

I brought anointing oil and touched Logan's forehead every morning. I whispered Psalm 91 over him—the very Scripture that had always brought us comfort:

"For He shall give His angels charge over you,
to keep you in all your ways."
—Psalm 91:11

And I believed it. With all my heart.

The angel in the painting. The feather at Lisa's feet. The voice Logan heard in the car. The unseen hand holding him upright as he walked through the ER doors.

God had assigned His angels to my son.

And though we were surrounded by machines, tubes, alarms, and uncertainty, there was a divine calm in that room.

Because Heaven was there.

Chapter 4: The Ministry of Presence

There are hospital rooms…

And then there are places where Heaven and Earth touch.

Logan's ICU room was one of those places.

From the moment I stepped in, I knew we weren't just walking into a medical crisis. We were stepping into a holy appointment. The machines hummed, the monitors beeped, and the fluorescent lights cast their usual glare—but none of that could drown out the quiet presence of the Lord.

You could feel Him there.

Even the doctors and nurses said it.

They'd pause before speaking.

Whisper instead of talking.

Several of them said things like, "There's peace in here," or "This room feels holy."

One nurse, eyes misting, simply said, "God is in this room."

And He was.

Every breath, every heartbeat Logan clung to was held in God's hands. And I clung to Him too—with everything I had.

Lisa and I stayed by Logan's side, day and night.

I read Psalm 23:4 over him again:

"Even though I walk through the valley of the shadow of death,
I will fear no evil, for You are with me;
Your rod and Your staff, they comfort me."

Psalms 23:4

And I sang.

Even when my voice shook, I sang.

"Love of God" by Phil Wickham and Brandon Lake, and "Hymn of Heaven" by Phil Wickham became my offering—my lullaby, my prayer, my surrender. I sang those songs over Logan every single day he was in the ICU.

Sometimes I'd stand beside him, hand on his arm, singing through tears.

Other times I'd sit in the recliner, staring at the angel in the left corner of the painting on the wall, knowing—just knowing—Logan's guardian was still near.

I wasn't alone.

I stayed in constant contact with my best friend and prayer warrior, Debra from church. She prayed with me faithfully, lifting Logan up with bold belief that God could still perform a miracle. I begged God to take me instead of Logan, but that wasn't part of His plan.

Our prayers were full of faith, not fear.

We didn't just pray for comfort.

We prayed for healing.

We prayed that God would breathe life back into Logan's body. That he would rise with power. That his testimony would not end in this hospital room.

And then, on the second day, something happened that would mark us forever.

A tall man walked into the room—calm, quiet, purposeful.

He wore green scrubs. No name tag. His curly hair hung around his shoulders. He said nothing else—just gently stepped to Logan's bedside and looked down at him.

"I'm Dr. Mordecai," he said softly. "The liver doctor."

Then he placed his hand on Logan and whispered:

"You know the liver can regenerate itself, right?"

That was all.

No small talk. No chart. No questions.

Just that one, hopeful sentence.

He stood on the left side of Logan's bed, near me. And then something strange happened—a nurse nearly backed into him... but didn't react.

She hadn't seen him at all.

At that moment, nine doctors entered the room—Logan's care team. They lined up along the wall near the doorway. Not one of them acknowledged Dr. Mordecai. They didn't nod. Didn't speak. Didn't even glance in his direction.

Then, calmly, Dr. Mordecai walked right in front of them and left the room—unnoticed, untouched, unseen.

An hour later, a surgeon entered to update us. I asked her directly, "Who was that doctor in here earlier? The one who said he was Dr. Mordecai?"

She blinked in confusion. "What doctor?"

I repeated myself. "Dr. Mordecai. He said he was the liver doctor."

She shook her head. "There's no Dr. Mordecai at this hospital… and none at the liver transplant center nearby either."

Lisa and I locked eyes.

We didn't need an explanation.

We knew.

Logan's angel had returned.

On day five, he came again.

He entered just as quietly, just as calmly.

He touched Logan's stomach gently and said:

"They need to look somewhere else. There's nothing here."

Then he turned to leave the room.

At that moment, a radiologist was entering to check the machines. He and Dr. Mordecai brushed shoulders in the doorway.

Lisa quickly asked him, "Who was that doctor leaving just now?"

He looked at her, confused.

"There was no one coming out as I walked in."

She said, "You brushed shoulders with him!"

Still confused, the radiologist replied, "There was no one else there."

But we knew better.

We'd been visited by Logan's guardian angel, again.

He had come to reassure us.

To offer peace.

To gently guide us through the valley of shadows.

And that was the last time we ever saw Dr. Mordecai.

He never returned to Logan's room again.

But his presence never really left.

Chapter 5: Crossing Over

Saturday, September 28, 2024.
The final day of Logan's seven-day journey.
The day Heaven opened its arms.
The day my world broke… and was somehow held by God at the same time.

At 1:30 AM, a doctor walked into Logan's ICU room with a glimmer of hope.
He said Logan was looking better. His numbers were improving. He was breathing over the ventilator.
They were planning to take him off the machine later that morning to see if he could breathe on his own.

I clung to that news like a lifeline.
Maybe—just maybe—God was answering our prayers for a miracle.

I curled up in the recliner close to Logan's bed and let myself rest for a moment, my spirit both weary and cautiously hopeful.

Then at 8 AM, I was suddenly awakened by something unmistakable.

Logan's cologne.

It filled the air around me—strong, familiar, comforting. But he hadn't worn cologne in weeks… and fragrances weren't even allowed in the ICU.

Before I could process it, I looked over and saw Lisa waking up.
I turned to her and said, "You're not going to believe what I—"
She interrupted me mid-sentence, eyes wide.
"You smelled his cologne too, didn't you?"
We stared at each other, tears welling.

In that moment, we both knew—deep in our hearts—Logan's spirit had just left his body.

We knew he had gone Home.

But our minds… our mother-hearts… were still holding on. Still hoping. Still praying for one more miracle.

By 3 PM, the doctors returned and told us they needed to run one final test.

They asked us to leave the room for an hour or so. If the test didn't work, things wouldn't look good.

Still holding on to hope, Lisa and I left and went downstairs to get some fresh air.

We took the elevator down, and as we rode together, I joked to Lisa that my purse was getting too heavy.

I laughed, "when I get home, I'm taking all the change out of my wallet."

It was a moment of levity in a day heavy with sorrow.

Outside, the hospital entrance was buzzing. At least 60 to 100 people stood waiting, some for rides, some for air, some for answers.

Lisa and I found a quiet spot off to the left, away from the crowd.

I called my sister, Vickie, and began giving her the latest update.

That's when I saw a man approach Lisa.

After a few minutes she tapped my shoulder and whispered, "I don't understand what he's saying."

I quickly ended my call and turned to the man.

He looked lost. Broken. Worn down.

"I just lost my entire family in a wreck," he told us. "I'm trying to get home to my parents… but they're elderly and can't come get me. Do you have any change?"

I couldn't believe what I was hearing.

I smiled and told him, "I was just telling Lisa in the elevator that I had so much change in my purse, and it was hurting my shoulder to carry it."

I opened my wallet and began pouring coins into his hand—happy to help—but then I saw them.

Two special coins I had completely forgotten about:

My guardian angel coin.

And Logan's St. Michael's coin.

I gently pulled them back from the pile.

"We're going to need these when we go back upstairs," I told Lisa, quietly.

Then I handed the man a few bills and said, "If you hadn't asked me for change, I wouldn't have remembered these coins were in my wallet."

He thanked me and turned to walk away.

And just like that—he disappeared into the crowd.

I felt something shift.

Like a whisper in my soul…

"Go back upstairs. Now."

We got into the elevator and as the doors opened on the ICU floor, two doctors were waiting for us—frantic, searching.

"There you are," one of them said as they pulled us aside. "The procedure didn't work. You have two hours to get your family here."

I nearly collapsed.

Even though my heart had already felt Logan leave, hearing those words shattered what was left of me.

I messaged Debra.

Told her Logan had two hours.

Her response was holy and hard.

"You need to change your prayer," she said.

"From 'God save my son's life' to 'God, please take my son home.'"

That message changed me.

Debra will never know how deeply she carried me during those seven days.

How her prayers steadied mine when my hands were shaking.

I called Logan's daddy, Cliff, and his wife Becky.

Told them the time had come. They need to hurry—and to tell the family to get there as fast as they could.

At **6:04 PM**, on **September 28, 2024**…

Logan was taken off the ventilator.

And he was pronounced dead.

I was in disbelief.

"He's gone," the doctor said.

But how?

How could my beautiful boy be gone?

I leaned over him, sobbing, as if my body could bring his back to life.

As if the weight of my grief could pull him from Heaven and place him back in my arms.

The chaplain came in.

We prayed Psalm 23:4.

The family surrounded Logan, speaking prayers and blessings over his sacred body.

And then, they left me alone.

I laid over Logan's body, broken, undone.

I wept until I had no strength left to cry.

And just when I thought I couldn't bear one more second of pain, a nurse walked in.

But she wasn't kind.

She was the coldest, rudest nurse I had encountered the entire time.

"I need these papers signed so I can go home," she said flatly.

I looked up, stunned.

"I'm grieving the passing of my son," I told her. "Can this wait?"

"It needs to be done now," she snapped.

Through my tears, I signed the papers and handed them back. And I returned to mourning my child.

I knew what this was.

It was the enemy's final attempt to rattle me.

To distract me.

To twist something sacred.

But God won.

Even in that moment of cruelty—God still had the victory.

Part II: The Valley of Grief
Chapter 6: When Heaven Spoke Back

When Logan was pronounced dead, I was in complete disbelief. I couldn't catch my breath. I couldn't accept it. I lay over him, screaming through tears, "No, he can't be gone. No, he can't be gone." I was begging God to wake me up from the nightmare.

The doctors told me I could stay as long as I needed, and I did. But even eternity wouldn't have been long enough to say goodbye.

Eventually, I knew I had to do the hardest thing I've ever done in my life—pull myself off my child… and walk away.

Before I left, I took one final picture of him. Not to be morbid. Not for anyone else. But because I had taken a picture of my son when he entered this world, I was going to take a picture of him as he left it. That was my sacred act of motherhood. The closing of a circle.

Lisa and I were too distraught to drive, so Logan's daddy, Cliff, drove my truck, with Becky and the family following behind. The whole ride home, we talked about Logan's life. We were stunned and confused about what had just happened. We couldn't believe that was the last time we'd ever see Logan again.

When I got home, I collapsed in bed and cried until I couldn't breathe.

And that's when I had what I now know was a visit from my mom, who had passed more than 20 years earlier. In this visitation, she crawled into bed beside me, lay next to me, and held my hand. She didn't say a word.

She didn't have to.

Her presence told me, *Logan is home… and he's safe.*

But then God gave me a gift.

A vivid image, like a screenshot in my mind.

I saw Logan standing on the other side of Heaven's gate, walking forward, but turning back to look at me with the biggest smile on his face.

He was glowing.

It was like he was saying, *"I made it, Mama."*

And that's when my heart truly knew—Logan was home.

The days that followed were unbearable.

I couldn't eat. Couldn't sleep. I didn't know who I was anymore. Without being Logan's mama, I felt lost. Empty.

But then… the signs began.

A few days after Logan passed, I walked out to the mailbox, still in a fog of grief. There's a cane bush near our mailbox—and I've never seen butterflies around it in the 10 years we've lived here.

But on that day, it was covered in 50 to 60 butterflies—bright, beautiful, dancing all around me like a living message from Heaven.

And I haven't seen a single butterfly on that bush since.

Then the feathers started to appear.

White feathers. Everywhere.

In places they had no business being:

– Spinning in the front seat of my truck where Logan used to sit
– Under the covers in Bryden's bed
– On the floor where Bryden had just been standing

I started collecting them. I keep them in a special container, and one day, I'll give them to Bryden when he's old enough to understand what they mean.

Then came the first real sign of Logan's presence, just a week after he passed.

A friend sent me a video from Bryden's 3rd birthday—taken the year before. I filmed it in our kitchen. Bryden was sitting in his highchair, giggling, and reaching toward the candle on his birthday cake.

Logan's arms were in the frame, guiding him gently.

Logan was saying, "No, Bubba. Hot." —because Bryden was trying to touch the flame on the candle.

Bryden repeated, "Hot."

It was just them. Pure and sweet.

As I watched the video, I was crying uncontrollably. I needed air. I walked outside with my dog, Thor.

If you know Scripture, you know:

Seven is God's number—perfection, holiness, completion.

Nine means finality, the end of a cycle.

That photo wasn't an accident.

It was a message from years ago—God whispering the future in advance.

Then, not long after, Brandon Lake released a song called *"Seven"* ... and I knew it was connected.

Logan was in the ICU for seven days.

A full, sacred, complete journey.

My sweet Bryden is what keeps me going.

He is Logan's identical twin in so many ways. The look in his eyes. His laugh. His presence. It's like Logan gave me a piece of himself to hold onto through his son.

We keep Logan alive in this house:

– We watch his videos

– We listen to his voicemails

– We talk about him daily

– We built a "Logan Wall" with photos and gifts people have given us in his memory

After the memorial, my dear friend Susanna told me, "Make a post about Logan every day for 365 days. On day 366, Facebook will begin showing them as memories forever."

So, I did.

And I will.

I'm saving them all to create a book for Bryden—his father's voice, love, and legacy captured in writing.

Then, about a month ago—nine months after Logan passed—God spoke to me again.

He told me to begin sharing Logan's story on YouTube. To speak about grief, hope, and Heaven.

And every day since, I've posted.

The messages I've received from strangers are proof—Logan is still touching lives from Heaven.

He doesn't have to be here physically to change the world.

Logan had an anointing on his life.

And now, God has placed a calling on mine—to keep his legacy alive.

I am Logan's mama.

I am Bryden's Naw-Naw.

And I will spend the rest of my life telling this story.

Because Logan's life had purpose.

Logan's death had holiness.

And Logan's legacy is eternal.

Chapter 7: Grace for the Empty Places

Logan passed away on Saturday, September 28, 2024. I thought that would be the hardest day of my life.

But then Sunday came—the first full day I had to live without my son.

He was 32 years old. I had 32 years with him by my side, and in a single moment, it felt like all of that was wiped away.

I was lost. I couldn't pray. I couldn't think. My brain was in a fog. My heart knew Logan was gone, but my mind wasn't accepting it. I stayed in bed, crying all day. I didn't want to talk to anyone or message anybody back. I couldn't even read texts that flooded in. Every message of condolence felt like another confirmation that this nightmare was real, and I just couldn't take it.

I kept waiting to wake up. I kept hoping it was all some kind of horrible dream.

But Sunday came and went, and Logan was still gone.

Monday: The Funeral Home

Monday brought a new wave of pain. I had to do the unthinkable. Lisa, Logan's girlfriend, his daddy Cliff, his stepmom Becky, and my sister-in-law Dana all came with me to the funeral home.

Sitting there, talking about my son's memorial service, choosing urns, and discussing cremation—it was surreal. I was in shock. I never imagined this moment. We went through flowers, the order of service, the costs of everything. We were choosing arrangements that we felt would represent Logan's life.

Cliff ordered a beautiful wreath with a barber pole in the center, honoring Logan's gift as a barber. Becky chose a breathtaking pair of angel wings made from white feathers. I picked out a beautiful floral arrangement from me, Amber and Lisa.

I had assumed I'd get to see Logan again before the cremation, but I was wrong. Because of how he was transported directly from the hospital to the crematorium in Houston, there was no viewing. No last look. That realization shattered me all over again. The last time I saw him was at the hospital. That was it.

No mother should ever have to go through that. The loss was heavy, like I couldn't breathe, like I was drowning in grief. I had no air and no way to come up for it.

Just two months before, Logan and I had casually talked about cremation, telling him what to do with my ashes when my time came. I never imagined I'd be handling his first.

Dana later told Lisa she was afraid I was going to go home and take my own life. And I'll be honest—I had a passing thought.

But God held me. Even in the valley, I could feel Him holding me up.

Tuesday: Urns, Plans, and a Heavy Heart

Tuesday was filled with more decisions. Cliff and I ordered custom urns with barber poles on them. They were stunning and felt so personal. Many friends and family members wanted a small part of Logan's ashes, so I carefully selected urn necklaces for me, Amber, and Lisa, and small urns for those I knew Logan would want to have them.

I called my church, Harvest Church in Jasper, to ask if we could hold Logan's memorial there. I wanted him to be sent off in the house of the Lord. They agreed, and I asked if Pastor Gary Marshall could speak. I knew no one else could do it the way he could.

But Pastor Gary and Pastor Karen were out of the country. My heart sank. I couldn't imagine anyone else leading the service. Thankfully, when I messaged Pastor Karen, she told me they would be back late Saturday night. Pastor Gary offered to lead the memorial after church service on Sunday, October 6. It was a huge relief.

I went to church that Sunday morning, holding myself together by a thread. My heart was screaming, "Why, God? Why?"

Logan's Memorial Service

After church, the team from the mortuary began setting up. Friends and family joined to help prepare the photo tables. Seeing Logan's life laid out like that was excruciating. It was a visual summary of his entire life, each picture a reminder that he was no longer here.

About 100 people came. Just as many messaged me, saying they couldn't attend but were with us in spirit. Some people I didn't recognize, but there were friends from Logan's childhood or people whose lives he had quietly impacted.

When the service began, Cliff and I broke down. The grief filled the sanctuary. There were flowers lining the altar, and a 16x20 framed photo of Logan, taken the day he opened his barbershop, it sat on an easel. He looked so proud and sophisticated—exactly how I want to remember him.

We opened the service with a 20-minute slideshow of Logan's life—from the moment he took his first breath to the final days we held him here on earth. Each photo was a sacred thread in the story of his beautiful life, and as they played one after another, it felt like my soul was being torn in two. The pain was so deep, I truly thought I might collapse beneath the weight of it.

Then Pastor Gary stepped up. And in that unbearable ache, his presence became a lifeline. Every word he spoke felt like a steady hand holding mine, reminding me to breathe, to hold on, to believe that God was still nearby.

At one point, he paused and looked at Cliff and me—his eyes filled with compassion and tears—and he prayed for strength to fill our shattered hearts. He could see how undone we were in our grief, and his prayer felt like a covering—like God reaching down to hold us when we couldn't stand on our own.

After the service, people lined up to hug Cliff and me. I was so distraught I barely remember who came through the line. But I'm forever grateful to my husband, John. He held me up when I couldn't stand on my own.

Three long tables were filled with Logan's photos and memories. I'm so glad I was always that mama with a camera in his face, even when he rolled his eyes at me. Those moments are treasures now.

After the memorial, everyone gathered in the Life Center for food. The women from our church's hospitality team prepared an incredible spread. Their kindness and love carried me that day. I don't know if they'll ever understand how much their presence, kindness, and help meant to me.

Walmart and the Fog of Grief

For the first three months after Logan passed, I was deeply depressed. I only left the house to go to church. But one day, I decided to go to Walmart. I thought I could handle it—just in and out.

But in the middle of the store, grief ambushed me. I froze in an aisle, crying uncontrollably. I couldn't move. I stood there for 30 minutes while people walked by and stared at me. No one said a word. I felt invisible and completely alone in a store full of people.

Eventually, I unfroze, left my cart, ran out and sped home—right back to the same darkness and depression I'd tried to escape.

Bereaved Mamas and a New Resolve

Before Logan passed, God had been placing grieving mothers in my life. I see now that He was preparing me. Since Logan's death, even more bereaved mamas have been placed in my path—not by coincidence, but for comfort and connection. We hold space for one another in a way only another grieving mother can.

After about four months in that deep pit, I woke up one morning and said, "I'm not going to live like this anymore." God had blessed me with clarity—Logan's life mattered, and it was up to me to keep his legacy alive. For myself. For Bryden. For everyone who felt his love.

Spreading Logan's Light

Since the day after Logan's memorial, I've posted a photo and a message about him every single day on Facebook. My friend Susanna suggested I do it, and I'm so thankful she did. One day, I'll turn those posts into a book for Bryden.

Today marks Day 300.

In 65 more days, Logan will have been gone for a full year. Some days, I still feel like I'll wake up from this nightmare. Sometimes I stare at his photos too long and slip back into that denial. But I must snap out of it—because I won't go back to that pit of depression.

God has given me a gift: Bryden Lane Parsons.

He is Logan's twin—same look, same expressions, same spirit. When I look at him, I feel like I'm in a time machine.

I'll grieve Logan until my last breath, but God is doing a beautiful work in me. Because of Logan and the love, he gave, I now love deeper, hug longer, and live with greater purpose.

This is God's message, Logan's story—And I'm the voice.

I will keep doing God's will to carry Logan's legacy. He was chosen. And now, I have chosen to carry his light.

Logan is safe in the arms of Jesus, watched over by God.

How can I be sad or even mad about that?

God was with me in the valley—and He is with me now as I spread Logan's light to the world.

Chapter 8: Threads of Comfort in the Days After

Lisa and I stayed close during this time. She grieved not just as Logan's girlfriend, but as someone who truly loved him with her whole heart. The bond they shared was real and deep—and losing him broke something inside of her too. In the days after the memorial, we leaned on each other—sometimes crying, sometimes just sitting in silence, holding space for one another. No words were needed. Our hearts knew the weight of what had been lost.

The days following the memorial were a blur of stillness and movement. So many people reached out—bringing food, sending cards, offering hugs and prayers. I was beyond grateful... but I was also mentally and physically exhausted. Grief doesn't give you time to breathe. It just sits with you—quietly, constantly.

Sometimes, when I couldn't take the noise of the world, I'd go to Logan's house and just to sit. To smell his scent. To be near his things. Every item felt sacred—his cologne still sitting on the dresser, his shoes by the door just as he left them, even the empty wrappers from snacks he had once enjoyed. Nothing had moved. I couldn't bring myself to change a single thing. It was like I was frozen in time, clinging to anything that still carried his essence.

But in that thick, aching darkness, Bryden was my light.

He was two months shy of turning four years old when Logan passed—too young to understand the depth of what had happened, but somehow, he felt it. His little heart was connected to his daddies in a way I can't explain. He would look up at us with those big innocent eyes and ask for his daddy... and we didn't know how to answer. How do you explain eternity to a child? Our words felt too small. Too fragile.

Months passed, and one day Amber gently told me, "You can tell him Daddy's in Heaven." So, I did. And Bryden, in his sweet, childlike way, would nod like he understood. Then he'd run off to play, chasing butterflies or laughing at the sky. It shattered me every time… but it also reminded me that Logan wasn't just a memory in our hearts—he was still present, still moving through our lives in quiet, beautiful ways, especially in Bryden's life.

One morning, just a few days after the memorial, I walked into the kitchen to make some tea. The morning sun was pouring through the window in that golden, glowing way that reminded me of Logan's smile—warm, bold, full of life. I glanced down, and there on the floor by the back door was a small white feather. It hadn't been there the night before. No one had gone in or out. I knew—without a doubt—it was Logan. A whisper from Heaven. A reminder that he was still nearby.

Another day, Bryden and I went to the store, and out of nowhere he pointed to this big, colorful rainbow ball. "I need that ball," he said with such certainty.

I didn't know why, but I bought it for him. When we got home, we went into the backyard to play. He kicked that ball around like it was the best gift in the world—laughing, running, smiling from ear to ear. I asked him if I could kick it too, and without hesitation, he said firmly, "No. This is Daddy's ball."

I froze. I had never told him that. I hadn't said anything about Logan at that moment. But he knew.

From that day on, whenever Bryden comes to my house, the first thing he asks is, "Where's Daddy's ball?" And we go outside to play, and I watched him kick that ball, beaming with joy—and I know Logan is right there, in the yard with us. I can feel it in the air. I can see it in Bryden's face.

And then one day, Bryden looked up at the necklace I wear around my neck every day, the one that holds a tiny urn with Logan's ashes inside. He touched it gently and said, "That's Daddy's necklace."

With tears in my eyes, I whispered, "Yes, baby. That's Daddy's necklace."

I had never told him what was in it. But somehow, he knew.

I believe Logan told him. I believe his spirit whispered it gently into Bryden's heart: *I'm still with you. I'm still with Naw Naw. I haven't gone far.*

Moments like these—so simple, yet so sacred—remind me that Logan's story isn't over. It lives on in Bryden's laughter, in the feathers that appear from nowhere, in rainbow balls and quiet sunrises and innocent words spoken with Heaven in their breath. And though my heart aches every day, I hold on to these signs. These miracles. These whispers from above.

Because love like Logan's doesn't end. It just changes form.

And it keeps showing up… exactly when we need it most.

Chapter 9 – Faith That Holds the Broken

There's a kind of silence that follows deep silence that doesn't just settle in the room but inside your very soul. That was the silence I lived in after Logan's memorial. The busyness of funeral planning was over, the service had passed, and people slowly began to return to their own lives. But mine was forever changed. I was left alone with the echo of memories and the ache of a thousand unspoken prayers.

And yet—even in that silence—God was speaking.

I would often feel Logan near in the smallest, most tender ways. A feather left where no feather should be. The sudden scent of something that reminded me of him. A butterfly circled me for just a moment too long. These were not coincidences. These were reminders from Heaven. Love notes from my son. Assurances from my father.

There were days I still couldn't make sense of how the world kept turning. I'd go to church, raise my hands in worship, and still cry through every song. Some days I couldn't even stand. But the people at Harvest Church loved me through every trembling moment. My pastors, my friends—especially my prayer warrior, Debra—held me up when I couldn't stand on my own. And every time I thought I couldn't take another breath, God would send a word, a whisper, or a moment of peace that wrapped around me like a blanket.

I started keeping a journal—not just of grief, but of grace. I wrote down the ways God was showing up in my everyday life—through Bryden's giggles, through scriptures that popped up at just the right time, through unexpected phone calls, and through the strength He gave me to get up each day. Slowly, I began to see a purpose forming in the pain.

People began reaching out, other grieving mothers, families who had lost children, people who had followed Logan's story through

Facebook and YouTube. They'd tell me how Logan had impacted their lives, how his smile or his story had drawn them back to God. Some even said they started praying again because of him. That's when I knew this wasn't just grief. It was ministry.

God was calling me to something deeper—to speak, to write, to share. Not just about Logan's death, but about his life. His legacy. His light. I realized that if I kept quiet, then Logan's story would only stretch as far as my own heart. But if I opened, if I surrendered this pain to God, He could use it to reach the ends of the earth.

There is power in testimony. And mine begins and ends with Logan.

He was born into love, lived with compassion, and left with grace. And through every day that followed, God has taken my shattered heart and turned it into a vessel. I still grieve. I still cry. But I also praise. I also hope.

Because faith isn't about avoiding the fire—it's about trusting the One who walks through it with you.

I know without a shadow of a doubt: Logan walks with Jesus. And Jesus walks with me.

And when I can't take another step, when the weight of grief starts to press too heavy on my chest, I whisper these words into the silence that once scared me:

"God, I still believe."

Even in the ache.

Even in the questions.

Even when healing feels slow.

Because the same God who held Logan in his final breath… is the same God who's holding me now.

Part IV: The Road Map – God's Whisper Before the Storm

Chapter 10 – Premonitions and Divine Clues

In February of 2024, something in my life shifted.

I had walked through many storms in my life, but that month, I finally surrendered. I was tired of doing things with my own strength. And for the first time, I reached out to the One who had been waiting for me all along.

That was the beginning of my walk with God.

In May, on Mother's Day, I went to church for the very first time in many years.

Logan came with me and Amber a few times, and while he didn't like sitting through service, I never pushed him. I trusted that God would work in him just like He was working in me. Because what began in those early days was more than a spiritual awakening.

It was a divine conversation.

And God wasn't speaking through sermons or devotionals. He was speaking directly to me in the quiet moments just as I was waking up.

It wasn't an audible voice. It wasn't a dream.

It was like a movie screen in my mind—flashes of symbols, numbers, letters, words, images. At first, everything moved so fast I couldn't make sense of it. But over time, I began to see clearly.

And I knew—it was God.

I started writing everything down in a journal I call my *Premonition Book*.

The very first message came through on May 5, 2024. Just two words:

Heaven. Faith.

At the time, I thought God was telling me I needed to have faith because I was coming to Heaven.

But now I understand.

He was saying, *you'll need faith… because your son is coming to Me.*

From that day on, the messages continued. I didn't know what they meant—but I wrote everyone down.

I trusted that they weren't for anyone else.

They were for me.

And God was preparing my heart—one word at a time.

June 16

The word *Frazier* appeared. Just my last name, nothing more.

But in my spirit, I knew this wasn't just about me. It was about all of us. God was letting me know something was coming that would affect the whole Frazier family.

June 22

I saw a pencil sketch—a pair of eyes. Along with the words:

"Look for it."

I didn't know what to look for. I didn't try. I figured it would come to me when it was supposed to.

June 28

I saw one word: *Logan.*

I thought God was saying He was going to heal Logan. That He would set him straight, ease his struggles, break the anxiety and addiction. I stressed about Logan daily, begging God to help him and me.

Now I know… God was going to heal him.

Just not in the way I had imagined.

July 1

A message came through: *"Did you see it?"*

But I hadn't. I wasn't looking.

August 7

Three words appeared:

"Chapter. Me. Change."

I felt it deep down—a new chapter was coming. Something big. And I would have to change significantly for it.

August 21

A direct command:

"Make a change, Angela."

I wish I had listened. I was pushing hard to get an online business off the ground—something I thought would give me peace and freedom. But God wasn't in it.

Instead of letting go, I stayed in my office 24/7. I was exhausted, screaming at the computer, crying every night. My husband would come home and find me breaking down. One day he said, "Do you think God is telling you to STOP?"

Of course, I knew that was true. But I was determined to start this business no matter what.

If I had stepped away… I could have spent more time with Logan. With Bryden. With what truly mattered.

September 3

Five haunting words: *"He's not mine anymore."*

I didn't understand it then. But now I do.

God was saying, *He's coming home to Me.*

September 12

One word: *"Chosen."*

I thought that message was for me.

But it was for Logan.

He was Chosen. Set apart. Anointed.

I never looked back at anything I wrote.

Every day I just wrote what I saw. I didn't analyze it. I didn't try to interpret it. I just trusted that it was from God.

And then, five months after Logan passed, I opened my *Premonition Book.*

For the first time, I read through every entry.

And when I did…

It was like I was staring at a map.

A holy, heartbreaking, miraculous road map.

God had been preparing me for the inevitable.

Each word.

Each image.

Each date.

They weren't random.

They were breadcrumbs from Heaven, leading me through the valley I didn't yet know I'd Walk.

And now I see…

Even when I didn't understand,

God was already making a way.

Chapter 11 – The Messages Begin

When Logan passed, I thought the silence would be deafening.

I thought I'd never hear from him again.

That the world would just keep spinning without him.

That God's voice would go quiet in my grief.

But what happened instead was something sacred.

God spoke louder.

Logan spoke softer.

And the veil between Heaven and Earth became thinner than I'd ever imagined.

The first message came just weeks after Logan passed.

I was still heavy in grief—barely functioning, barely breathing.

And yet, God met me in the middle of my pain with the most unexpected comfort.

I was at a women's retreat with my church, just three weeks after Logan passed away, sitting outside with Debra. We were talking about Logan—how Lisa had seen the huge white feather the night she took him to the ER, how he still seemed to be with me in ways I couldn't explain.

Debra paused.

Then she looked at me and said, "Angela, turn around. Look up and tell me what you see."

I turned.

And in the sky behind me was a massive white feather—formed entirely from clouds.

It was perfect. Pure. Suspended in the blue.

I gasped.

It was the most beautiful thing I had ever seen.

In that moment, I knew—God was reminding me He was still with me. And so was Logan.

After that day, the signs only grew stronger.

On October 14, I was struggling deeply. Barely making it. My heart felt like it had been hollowed out.

That morning, two words came through:

Holy Bible.

Ephesians.

God knew I needed His Word. He knew I needed armor for the days ahead.

And I dove into Scripture like never before.

On October 18, just four days later, came another moment I'll never forget.

I had a visitation from Logan—not in a dream, but in a way only a mother can recognize.

It was quiet. Gentle. Loving.

And it carried a message of *Love*.

Then on November 29, these words came through:

"I love y'all so much every day."

I knew it was Logan.

There wasn't a doubt in my spirit.

It was him. Reaching from Heaven. Telling us what every grieving heart longs to hear:

That he still loves us.

That he still sees us.

That he's not gone—just gone Home.

And the messages didn't stop there.

Lisa's grandson, Huey, and Logan's son, Bryden, were both four years old.

And both of them… began seeing Logan.

Plain as day.

You could see it in their eyes.

In the way they stared off at nothing.

In the way they smiled mid-sentence when they talked to Logan.

In the way they carried on full conversations with someone only they could see.

One day, Huey pointed toward the air and said, "Da-da."

Lisa asked him, "Who are you talking to, baby?"

And he replied, calm as ever, "Da-da."

We believe with our whole hearts… he was talking to Logan—because that's what he called him.

Then came the first true visitation.

It was January 2, 2025.

I was lying on the couch, emotionally drained, unsure if I was asleep or awake.

And I felt a gentle tug on my hand.

My arm had been laid over my head, and the tug was soft—like Logan used to do when he needed me but didn't want to wake me.

Then I heard his voice:

"Are you awake, Mama?"

I whispered, "Yes… I'm awake."

And then it stopped.

I looked around.

No one was there.

But my heart was pounding.

Because I didn't just hear Logan…

I *felt* him.

The pressure of his hand. The familiarity of his presence.

On January 22, another message came through:

"GOD"—in bold, capital letters.

And then on January 28:

"Get ready for things to be shaken up."

And oh, how my life has been shaken up since then.

Everything turned upside down—but not in fear.

In faith.

In movement.

In calling.

I've had three or four visits since Logan passed.

Each one is beautiful. Real. Bittersweet.

In those moments, I can feel him:

Kissing my cheek

Wrapping his arms around me

Hugging me tight

Whispering, *"I love you, Mama. I miss you so much."*

And when I wake up?

I cry.

I scream.

I beg him not to go.

Because for a moment... I had him back.

And then... he's gone again.

But I know what these moments are.

They are proof.

That death doesn't end love.

That Heaven is closer than we think.

And that Logan is still living—in spirit, in signs, in legacy, in love.

Chapter 12 – The Signs After the Storm

It started with feathers.

Soft, white, impossibly placed feathers. They showed up in the most unexpected places where feathers just don't belong. At first, I thought maybe it was a coincidence. But as they kept appearing, I knew better. These weren't random. These were love notes from Heaven. These were Logan.

One of the first feathers I found was where Bryden was sleeping—tucked under the blanket, right beside him. Not on top where it might have floated, but underneath, nestled as if it had been placed there with care. It made no sense... unless it was divine. Unless it was a message.

Then I found one in the front seat of my truck. The seat where Logan always sat during our long drives. The feather was gently spinning in place, even though the windows were rolled up and no breeze could explain it. I sat there and watched it turn silent, sacred, steady. I felt peace wash over me. That feather was a whisper: *"I'm still with you, Mama."*

After that, the feathers began showing up more often—on Logan's "wall" of photos, in places Bryden would walk through on my Bible during prayer. Always white. Always clean. Always full of meaning.

But Logan didn't stop with feathers. The miracles began to multiply.

One day, Lisa and I were driving back through Jasper after dropping off Bryden. I ran into a small convenience store, leaving the truck running and praise music playing. When I came back out, Lisa was crying. She looked at me through tears and said, *"I didn't touch it. I didn't change anything."* I didn't understand at first—until I heard the voice coming from the speakers. It was Jim Gaffigan.

Comedy was our thing. Mine and Logan's. On road trips or errands, he'd always throw on Gaffigan routines, and we'd laugh till we cried. It was our little secret—just me, Logan, and God. Lisa had no idea. And yet, here it was, playing loud and clear, without anyone touching a thing. Then, when I put the truck in reverse, the music changed back to praise. Just like that.

It was Logan. I know it was.

And then there was the picture—the one my sister sent me on the 7-month anniversary of Logan's passing. I didn't even remember it being taken, but there they were: Logan and his cousin Lauren sitting on the couch. Lauren's shirt had the word *"Angel"* written across it, with a halo over the number *7*. And Logan's shirt? It was covered in number *9*.

Seven—God's number. Completion. Perfection. The number of divine purpose.

Nine—the biblical symbol of finality and fulfillment.

It was like a message from the past, echoing into my present: *"This journey was planned. It is finished. He is home."*

When Brandon Lake released the song *"Seven,"* it felt like confirmation. Logan had lived exactly seven days in the ICU. His journey wasn't just medical. It was miraculous. God had counted those days and marked them holy.

And now... the signs I receive aren't just for me. Something's changed.

At first, Logan's messages were gentle touches of comfort to help me survive the unspeakable. But now, they've become something greater. A call. A mission. I no longer keep them to myself—I share them. I post videos on YouTube. I write devotionals to give to people on a grief journey. I speak to others who are grieving. I tell Logan's story—because I know his voice still speaks from Heaven, and God is using it to reach hearts far beyond mine.

This chapter of my life—the one where Logan is no longer here in the flesh—isn't the end of our connection. It's the beginning of a new purpose. A purpose rooted in faith, forged in loss, and guided by miracles.

I collect Logan's feathers now. I keep them safe, tucked away in a special container. One day, I'll give them to Bryden when he's old enough to understand. When he's ready to know just how present his daddy still is in his life.

And maybe one day, when Bryden finds his own white feather lying somewhere it shouldn't be, he'll smile and say:

"Hi, Daddy. I know you're here."

www.ingramcontent.com/pod-product-compliance
Lightning Source LLC
Chambersburg PA
CBHW071633140626
46555CB00022B/2825